THE SECOND WORLD
IN PHOTOGR

1941

D. M. Meadows

January 2015

THE SECOND WORLD WAR AT SEA
IN PHOTOGRAPHS

1941

PHIL CARRADICE

AMBERLEY

First published 2014

Amberley Publishing
The Hill, Stroud
Gloucestershire, GL5 4EP

www.amberley-books.com

British Library Cataloguing in Publication Data.
A catalogue record for this book is available from the British Library.

ISBN 978 1 4456 2245 3 (print)
ISBN 978 1 4456 2268 2 (ebook)

Typeset in 10pt on 12pt Sabon.
Typesetting and Origination by Amberley Publishing.
Printed in the UK.

Contents

Introduction

The year 1941 started with mixed fortunes for Britain. In the first few days of January, the number of Luftwaffe aircraft in the Mediterranean rose to 270 bombers and forty fighters, a very real threat to the safety of British ships in the 'inland sea'. The German aircraft and aircrews offered a markedly different proposition from the more benign Italian air force.

As if to make the point, on 11 January the cruisers *Southampton* and *Gloucester*, en route to Gibraltar from the beleaguered island of Malta, were attacked by Stuka dive bombers. The *Southampton* was so badly damaged that she had to be sunk by a torpedo from the destroyer *Diamond*. She was the first of seven cruisers lost in the Mediterranean during 1941.

The same day, however, came the news that the catapult ship *Pegasus* had managed to launch a Sea Hurricane from her deck. This was the first operational launch of a fighter aircraft from such a ship. The use of aircraft flying from merchant ships was a welcome addition to the armoury of the convoy escorts, but it required a peculiar brand of courage from the pilots, as there was no way back to the launch ship and they had to be prepared to ditch in the sea once their patrol was over.

The news, in the early part of the year, that the USA was going to build 200 new freighters for use on the North Atlantic convoys – Liberty Ships as they soon became known – was a welcome fillip for the hard-pressed Merchant Marine. The ships might have been 'jerry built', their plates being spot welded rather than riveted, but over the next five years these large and often cumbersome cargo vessels played a vital role in supplying Britain with the food and materials required to keep fighting.

Between 1941 and 1945, a total of 2,710 Liberty Ships were built, American shipyards eventually turning them out in just forty-five to fifty days. President Franklin Delano Roosevelt declared that they were 'dreadful looking objects', but with assembly line production and a prefabricated hull, the ships were a crucial weapon in the Battle of the Atlantic. The Liberty Ships were supposed to have a life span of just five years – many of them lasted a lot, lot longer than that.

On 6 March, Winston Churchill made his famous remark, 'We must assume that the Battle of the Atlantic has begun.' It may have escaped his notice, but the Royal and Merchant Navies had been fighting that battle for many months. What is clear, however, is that from the beginning of 1941, the war in the Atlantic began to assume very dangerous proportions.

Churchill was later to say that the prospect of losing the Battle of the Atlantic was the one thing that frightened him during the war. He, like many others, knew that the German U-boats had a grip on Britain's throat and were slowly choking the lifeblood out of the country. It was the one battle Britain could not afford to lose.

For a long while in 1941 it really did seem as if Britain would lose the convoy/submarine war. And it was not just U-boats that caused the damage.

On 12 February, the unescorted convoy SLS-64 was attacked by the *Admiral Hipper*, nine of the convoy being sunk or seriously damaged in the encounter. On the 22nd of the same month, the battlecruisers *Scharnhorst* and *Gneisenau*, with Admiral Lutjens in charge, managed to frighten a convoy into scattering – they then proceeded to sink five of the merchantmen before refuelling at sea and heading for the west coast of Africa.

The German surface raiders, auxiliary steamers and cargo boats that had been created quietly and without fuss in the years immediately following the First World War also now came into their own. By 1941, ships like the *Pinguin*, *Thor* and *Atlantis* had been armed with guns – even catapult aircraft – and were roaming the oceans, destroying lone merchantmen and, perhaps more importantly, tying up valuable and much-needed warships to hunt them down.

In general, however, it was the U-boats that were in the van of battle and in the winter of 1941, Günther Prien, destroyer of the *Royal Oak* and hero of the U-boat service, was back in the thick of the action out in the Atlantic.

Having already sunk three of the merchant ships with his torpedoes, on 26 February Prien guided his submarine *U-47*, unnoticed, to the surface and began shadowing convoy OB-290. Sensing the opportunity for serious destruction, Prien called in the Luftwaffe and eleven ships from the convoy were sunk in the most successful air attack on Allied shipping to that date.

There were many other serious problems for both the Royal and Merchant Navies during 1941. The most significant of these can be highlighted as follows:

Defeating the Italian navy in the Mediterranean
The evacuation from Crete
Sinking of the *Hood*
The hunt for the *Bismarck*
The loss of the *Ark Royal*

Defeating the Italian navy was a priority and in admirals Somerfield and Cunningham the Admiralty had the right men for the job. At the Battle of Cape Matapan on 28 March, Cunningham came face to face with Admiral Angelo Iachino. The Italian fleet, consisting of one battleship, eight cruisers and over a dozen destroyers, had been drawn out of port by false reports that the Luftwaffe had disabled a number of British battleships. It was exactly the sort of mistake for which Cunningham had been waiting.

Cunningham engaged his enemy at long distance and the Italians promptly withdrew. Swordfish aircraft from the carrier *Formidable* then launched nine strikes against the Italian fleet, damaging the flagship *Vittoro Veneto* and bringing the cruiser *Pola* to a dead stop. Returning to help their damaged compatriots, the Italians ran into the whole Mediterranean fleet with the result that the *Pola* and two other cruisers, along with two destroyers, were sunk. It was a significant, morale-boosting victory for Cunningham and the Royal Navy.

The evacuation of the British and Allied armies from Crete was, ultimately, successful but at a terrible cost. Allied troops had been occupying Crete since October 1940, the island's ports offering the Royal Navy good bases in the eastern Mediterranean. In the wake of the German victory in Greece, the strategic importance of Crete was hammered home to British military planners. It was clear to everyone that Crete would be next.

The Battle for Crete began on 20 May. Initial German paratroop attacks on the island were costly but a badly handled defence saw Allied troops lose control of the airfields. Fighting desperately, they were gradually pushed back and eventually a decision to evacuate the island was made.

German attempts to disrupt the evacuation were thwarted by the Navy, but the vulnerability of stationary ships to aerial attack was soon evident. The battleships *Warspite* and *Valiant* were both badly damaged while the cruisers *Gloucester*, *York* and *Fiji* were hit by bombs and sunk.

When the ships of the 5th Destroyer Flotilla under Louis Mountbatten were ordered from Malta to help in the operation, they came under immediate air attack with the result that both the *Kashmir* and the *Kelly* were sunk. Cunningham signalled to the Admiralty that, because of the overwhelming superiority of German air power, daylight operations could no longer be sustained. His advice was ignored and the evacuation proceeded.

The withdrawal was eventually completed by 1 June, the cruiser *Calcutta* joining the casualty list. In all over 18,000 Allied troops were taken off the island but a further 17,000, many of them Anzac troops from New Zealand and Australia, were captured and forced to spend the rest of the war in German or Italian prison camps.

The sinking of the battlecruiser *Hood* on 24 May could not have come at a worse time, with the casualty figures from Crete rising by the hour. The *Hood*, pride of the British fleet, was blown apart when she and the newly completed *Prince of Wales* intercepted the *Bismarck* and *Prinz Eugen* in the Denmark Strait. The shock of the sinking – just three men saved from a total crew of 1416 – led to a national outcry and the call to 'Sink the *Bismarck*!'

The *Bismarck*, then the most powerful warship in the world, had sustained slight damage in the encounter with the two British ships and Admiral Lutjens decided to head for Brest, where his ship could undergo repairs. By now the hunting fleet was a significant force, including the battleships *King George V*, *Rodney* and *Ramillies* as well as the aircraft carrier *Victorious*. A detachment from Force H at Gibraltar, comprising the carrier *Ark Royal* and battlecruiser *Renown*, were also soon added to the fleet.

Torpedo attacks by Swordfish aircraft on 26 May damaged the *Bismarck*'s rudder and left her virtually helpless, capable only of steering in a circle. Lutjens and Hitler had decided that the *Bismarck* must fight to the death and when Admiral Tovey's *KGV* and *Rodney* – now almost out of fuel – finally intercepted her it was an action that could have only one outcome.

Pummelled by the shells of the British battleships, torpedoes from the cruisers *Norfolk* and *Dorsetshire* finally despatched the *Bismarck*, her crew assisting in her demise by scuttling their ship. There were only a few survivors, many of the crew having been killed in the battle and a U-boat alarm causing the British ships to break off the rescue attempt and head for port.

The Germans had claimed to have sunk the *Ark Royal* several times. They finally achieved it on 13 November when torpedoes from the U-81 ripped into her hull. She sank off Gibraltar the next day although it is now thought that better damage control might have saved the ship. Later in the month the battleship *Barham* was torpedoed, also in the Mediterranean. She blew up just five minutes after the torpedo struck, the first British battleship lost in open sea since the *Britannia* was sunk back in November 1918.

***

The sea war in 1941 was long and arduous as the battle against the U-boats grew in intensity. There were many desperate moments for the Royal and Merchant Navies with escorts and merchant ships – as well as many German submarines – going to the bottom on a regular basis. However, two events that seemed at the time to be just two more disasters that were guaranteed to produce greater hardships for all concerned, did actually have a significance that surpassed all understanding. They were events that affected the outcome of the war.

First came Hitler's invasion of Russia, Operation Barbarossa as it was properly known. Launched on 22 June, the sudden and unexpected attack on a country with which Hitler had recently signed a non-aggression pact involved German soldiers advancing on a 2,000 mile front. At first the German juggernaut simply steam-rollered everything in its path and there were moments when it seemed as if Russia was doomed.

Hitler, like everyone else, underestimated the strength of Russian determination and while it took time, his invasion simply underlined what he had always preached: the stupidity of fighting a war on two fronts. Starting on 21 August, British convoys to supply the Russians with weapons and armaments saw some of the heaviest and most bitter naval fighting of the war. A combination of the Russian weather and Russian determination brought the USSR to victory. Ultimately, Operation Barbarossa was the costliest mistake Hitler ever made.

The second event, one of major significance to world affairs, was the Japanese attack on the American fleet at Pearl Harbor. It was sheer chance but the American aircraft carriers were at sea on that day, otherwise the attack would have resulted in total victory for the Japanese. As it was, the American Pacific Fleet was sorely crippled and for many months there were very real fears of a Japanese invasion of the western coast of America.

The unexpected and unprovoked airborne assault, launched on 7 December 1941, may well have been, as President Roosevelt described it, 'a moment of infamy'. However, it also, as Admiral Yamamoto, the Japanese commander, may or may not have said, did nothing more than 'waken a sleeping giant'.

The attack brought the USA into the war. There were to be mistakes and defeats for the USA and her new Allies in the weeks and months ahead, but, eventually, the entry into the conflict of America with all the raw and latent industrial power she possessed virtually guaranteed the defeat of the Axis powers.

An aerial photograph of HMS *King George V*.

January

The mighty guns of HMS *Warspite*. On 3 January, the *Warspite*, along with the battleships *Valiant* and *Barham*, bombarded the Italian-held port of Bardia in Libya, a stronghold that had been holding up the British advance along the northern coast of Africa. British troops went on to capture the town two days later.

Above: On 11 January the cruisers *Southampton* and *Gloucester* were attacked by German aircraft, 180 miles off Malta. The *Southampton* was set on fire and so badly damaged that she had to be destroyed by a torpedo from the destroyer *Diamond*. The *Southampton* was the first of seven cruisers lost in the Mediterranean during 1941.

Opposite above: Commissioned in 1940, the carrier *Illustrious* was a vital part of the Mediterranean fleet. During an action off Pantellaria on 10 January 1941, her Chaplain, Henry Morgan Lloyd, won the DSO. It was the only DSO won by a naval chaplain during the Second World War. Lloyd lived until the ripe old age of ninety-nine.

Opposite below: The *Illustrious* is shown here in action against German and Italian bombers during the battle off Pantellaria in the straits between Sicily and the Italian mainland.

Above: A Sea Hurricane is shown here on the deck of a CAM ship. The acronym CAM ship stands for Catapult Aircraft Merchant Ship, a stop-gap attempt to provide air cover for convoys until enough escort carriers could be built. Pilots knew that they would either have to ditch in the sea or parachute clear of their aircraft – one launch was all that the ship and plane could manage. The first successful launch of a fighter from a CAM ship came on 11 January 1941 when a Hurricane was catapulted from the deck of the *Pegasus*.

Opposite bottom: HMS *Ark Royal*, HMS *Renown* and another battleship, off the Rock of Gibraltar.

The battleship *Prince of Wales* was commissioned on Sunday 19 January. It was to be the shortest commission of any British battleship before or since as the *Prince of Wales* was lost before the year was out.

The monitor *Terror* – a coastal bombardment vessel of First World War vintage – along with the gunboats *Gnat* and *Ladybird*, bombarded Tobruk, then in the hands of Italian forces, on 21 January. The British ships were part of the newly formed Inshore Squadron, commanded by Captain H. Hickling. The port of Tobruk surrendered to British and Anzac soldiers the following day.

The destroyer *Huntley* was attacked by Italian torpedo aircraft off the coast of Libya on 31 January. She sank within a few hours.

February

On 2 February aircraft from HMS *Ark Royal* attacked the power plant on Sardinia in what was known as Operation Picket. On the same day Fairey Albacore aircraft of 826 and 829 Squadrons Fleet Air Arm, flying from HMS *Formidable*, launched attacks on Mogadishu.

Albacores and Fulmars taking off from the carrier *Formidable*. The battleship in the background is the *Warspite*.

Opposite top: On 9 February, Force H under Admiral Somerville bombarded Genoa. The battleship *Malaya* and the *Renown* were part of the attacking group. A simultaneous attack was launched by aircraft from *Ark Royal* on Spezia.

Opposite bottom: The battleship *Malaya*, from Force H.

478/10   H.M.S. "MALAYA" INVERGORDON

The monitor *Terror* was badly damaged by bombs from Italian aircraft on 23 February. Despite attempts to save her, it was clearly a hopeless task and she was scuttled just 20 miles off the Libyan coast. There were no casualties. The *Terror* was the only British monitor to be lost during the war.

Opposite top: An artist's impression of the attack on Genoa on 9 February.

Opposite bottom: On 25 February, a single torpedo from the submarine *Upright* was enough to sink the Italian cruiser *Armando Diaz*. She went down a few miles off the coast of Tunisia.

On 27 February, the New Zealand cruiser *Leander* intercepted and sank the Italian raider *Ramb 1* in the Indian Ocean – after this, the Italians rarely used disguised raiders again.

Opposite top: The submarine *Snapper* was sunk on 11 February, just south of Ushant. A total of fifty-six depth charges were dropped on the submarine from three German minesweepers. The *Snapper* was the first of twelve large Royal Navy submarines lost in 1941.

Opposite bottom: An artist's impression of a patrol ship shooting down a German aircraft.

March

Operation Claymore was a joint operation involving five destroyers, two cross-Channel steamers, 500 men of 3 and 4 Commando and troops from Norway. With ships leaving port on 1 March, the attack took place three days later. The intention was to raid and destroy oil factories in the Lofoten Islands off the Norwegian coast.

The view from HMS *Legion* as the Lofoten oil tanks burn and blaze. The raid began at 0500 hours and was finished early in the afternoon. One bonus, hardly expected when the raid was planned, was the discovery of Enigma rotors taken when the trawler *Krebs* was captured during the raid.

Opposite bottom: Soldiers watching happily as the oil tanks on the Lofoten Islands burn. The raid took the German defenders totally by surprise. The tanks were destroyed, a fish factory ship was sunk and 200 prisoners taken. Psychologically, the raid was an enormous success – a chance to hit back at an enemy who had previously been victorious nearly everywhere.

A British destroyer on patrol in the Arctic.

It was not all gloom and doom in the convoy war and there was some success for the Royal Navy when, on 7 March, U-boat ace Günther Prien was killed when his submarine was depth charged by the destroyer *Wolverine*.

U-47, Prien's famous submarine, is shown here alongside the *Scharnhorst*. Prien was attacking OB-293 when he was surprised and forced to dive. Try as he might, he could not evade the hunting *Wolverine*. He was mourned as a national hero in Germany. British sailors might have respected his skill, but they were certainly glad to see him go.

An artisr's impression of a trawler shooting down a bomber.

A merchant ship ties up in port.

Opposite top: The Italian cruiser *Zara*, sunk in the Battle of Cape Matapan, which involved carrier-borne aircraft and big gun battleships.

Opposite bottom: The cruiser *Pola* was disabled by air attack and then sunk by gunfire in the final stages of the battle, along with the *Fiume* and two destroyers. The British lost just one aircraft, leaving Admiral Cunningham with a decisive victory. After his success at Taranto the previous year, the victory marked Cunningham as the pre-eminent British admiral of the war.

Top: The aircraft carrier *Formidable* provided the base for fighters and torpedo bombers to attack the Italian fleet. In all, she launched nine separate strikes and seriously damaged the Italian flagship *Vittorio Veneto* as well as bringing the cruiser *Pola* to a dead stop.

Above: The three Italian cruisers sunk at the Battle of Cape Matapan. Left to right: *Pola*, *Zara* and *Fiume* are shown here, moored securely in port before the fight.

With the German army making significant advances in Greece, naval activity around the Greek islands began to intensify in the spring of 1941. On 26 March, while anchored in Suda Bay in Crete, the cruiser *York* was hit by an Italian motor boat packed with explosives. Critically damaged, she was beached and later destroyed by attacks from German aircraft.

On 22 March the *Scharnhorst* and *Gneisenau* re-entered French waters. Despite desperate British attempts to intercept the two battlecruisers, they had, in a brief sortie, accounted for twenty-two merchant ships – some 115,600 tons of shipping. Had the German U-boat fleet been larger and able to work in conjunction with the surface ships, the losses would have been much greater.

British battleships *Barham*, *Valiant* and *Warspite* open fire on the Italian cruisers at the Battle of Cape Matapan.

A photograph of a message being passed by line while at sea. The cruiser has been camouflaged..

Continuous shipbuilding was important to the war effort. As one ship is being launched, work on another is begun.

Admiral Cunningham, victor at Cape Matapan.

The *Oder* was one of several large freighters built for the German merchant marine in the days when the country was not allowed a significant battle fleet. Like her contemporaries she had been built to be converted into an armed raider. However, her time as a raider was short lived and on 23 March 1941 she was intercepted by the sloop *Shoreham* in the Red Sea. With the situation clearly hopeless, the crew of the *Oder* scuttled their vessel.

U.S.S. Nevada, Port Angeles Harbor

The powerful American battleship USS *Nevada*.

The crew of an anti-aircraft gun on a destroyer take aim.

Admiral Günther Lutjens, who commanded the *Scharnhorst* and *Gneisenau* on their expedition into the North Atlantic, before he was appointed to overall command of the *Bismarck* and *Prinz Eugen*. The original German plan was to give him the *Tirpitz* and the two battlecruisers as well as the *Bismarck* – it would have been a formidable squadron.

April

On 3 April Swordfish aircraft from No. 813 and 824 Squadrons, Fleet Air Arm, attacked and sank two Italian submarines off Port Sudan. On the same day, two other enemy ships were attacked by RAF Wellington bombers and forced to scuttle.

The Armed Merchant Cruiser *Voltaire* was sunk in action with the German raider *Thor* on 4 April. With the *Voltaire* a blazing inferno, the *Thor* managed to rescue nearly 200 out of the British vessel's crew of 296.

The *Thor* enjoyed two highly successful raiding cruises before making for Japan, where she was destroyed in an accidental fire in 1942.

The old river gunboat *Gnat*, which took part in the bombardment of the coastal road near Bomba in Libya on 11 April, was, like many of the shallow draught river craft, already out of date when war began. Nevertheless, she carried out useful work along the North African coast.

On 15 April 1941, RAF Coastal Command came under the operational control of the Admiralty. It meant that aircraft like the giant Sunderland flying boats, although still flown by RAF crews, were guided and deployed by the Navy.

Right: Operation Demon, the evacuation of British and Allied troops from Greece, began on 24 April. It was completed by the 29th of the month. This shows exhausted British soldiers on the deck of a warship, headed towards what they clearly hope is a safe haven.

Below: The gunboat *Aphis* was part of the Inshore Squadron operating along the North African coast. She assisted the *Gnat* in her bombardment of the road near Bomba in early April.

The *Wryneck*, which was sunk alongside the *Diamond* on 27 April. The two destroyers had just picked up 700 soldiers – only fifty survived the bombing.

Right: With British soldiers being forced back by German attacks in North Africa, only the port of Tobruk managed to hold out. The siege of Tobruk lasted for over 200 days, the defending forces being supplied by the Royal and Merchant navies.

Below: The destroyer *Diamond*, sunk by German bombers off Nauplia on 27 April.

The Italian cruiser *San Giorgio* was disabled when the British first took Tobruk. Anti-aircraft guns were mounted on her deck and she was used as an independent fortress within Tobruk harbour. Before the port fell to the Germans the *San Giorgio* was again badly damaged and set on fire. Scuttled by the crew, she sank soon afterwards.

Right: Supplying the beleaguered garrison of Tobruk quickly became the primary concern of the Royal Navy. Warships and merchantmen were used for this vital task.

Below: An artist's impression of the British attack at Tobruk.

The submarine *Ultimatum*, a U class vessel, sister ship to the *Usk*, which was lost at the end of April 1941 within one year of her launch. No wreckage was ever found and her loss remains a mystery.

May

On 7 May, the German weather ship *München* was captured off Iceland. Importantly, the sailors who boarded her discovered the secret German Enigma keys for June. The captured *München* is seen here alongside the destroyer *Somali*.

The *Pinguin* was the most successful of all German surface raiders, capturing over thirty ships. She also seized the Norwegian whaling fleet, along with its catch, an operation condemned by Britain as an act of piracy! The *Pinguin* was one of the freighters laid down long before the war and destined for conversion into commerce raiders. The *Pinguin*'s highly successful career came to an end when she was intercepted and sunk by the *Cornwall* in the Indian Ocean on 8 May.

British cruisers on patrol in the Mediterranean.

The gunboat *Ladybird*, part of the Inshore Squadron, was bombed and sunk by German aircraft off the Libyan coast on 12 May.

Above: HMS *Hood*, the most famous ship in the Royal Navy, was sunk by the *Bismarck* on 24 May. The German battleship, in company with the heavy cruiser *Prinz Eugen*, was under orders to break for the North Atlantic, where she hoped to raid commerce and destroy as many convoys as possible. Shadowed, tracked and her location passed on by the cruisers *Norfolk* and *Suffolk*, the Admiralty confidently expected the battlecruiser *Hood* and the new, untried *Prince of Wales* to intercept and bring the *Bismarck* to battle. The possibility that the *Bismarck* might win the ensuing encounter did not enter anyone's head.

Opposite bottom: The destroyer *Kelly*, under the command of Lord Louis Mountbatten, had enjoyed an adventurous war. By rights she should have been sunk several times. To those on board – and to the general public – she seemed to have a charmed life, but her end finally came on 23 May when she was sunk by German aircraft 13 miles south of Gavdo.

Opposite top: With the situation on Crete growing worse by the minute, a decision was taken to evacuate the island – enter the Navy! This shows British warships, their decks packed with troops, off the coast of Crete.

Admiral Lutjens, commander of the German task force; together with the *Bismarck*'s captain, Ernst Lindemann, he was the driving force behind the German plan, Operation Rheinübung as it was known, to destroy Allied shipping in the North Atlantic. The *Bismarck*, along with her sister ship *Tirpitz*, was the most powerful battleship in the German navy, possibly even the world, and the need to prevent her escaping into the Atlantic was clear to everyone in the Royal Navy.

With Allied forces evacuated from Greece, it was obvious that the Greek islands would be next on the Germans' list. Many of the soldiers evacuated from mainland Greece went immediately to the island of Crete, where, it was soon clear, their respite was only temporary. The Battle for Crete duly began on 20 May and lasted until the final Allied soldiers were evacuated or captured on 1 June. This shows British ships under air attack in Suda Bay.

The *Hood*, a First World War veteran, was no match for the *Bismarck* and the Admiralty quickly put her destruction – as they did after the loss of the battlecruisers at Jutland in the First World War – down to weak deck armour. It is more likely that one of the *Bismarck*'s shells hit an ammunition store.

On the same day that the *Hood* was sunk, Lt
Cmdr Malcolm David Wanklyn, commander of
the submarine *Upholder*, was awarded the Victoria
Cross for bravery. The award made him the most
famous British submariner of the war.

The *Bismarck* opens fire on the *Hood* – her shooting was accurate and devastating. Only three of
the *Hood*'s crew of 1,416 survived. The *Prince of Wales*, brand new and with many dockyard maties
still on board, could do nothing as the *Hood* exploded in a mass of flames. She was lucky to escape
destruction herself.

The hunt for the *Bismarck* now assumed 'revenge proportions' – public opinion and naval pride decreed that the destruction of the *Hood* could not be allowed to go unpunished and a large array of warships was assembled to hunt her down.

Despite being low on fuel, the British battleships finally caught up with the *Bismarck* and soon the German ship was ablaze from stem to stern.

Opposite top: Rodney and *Ramillies* were just two of the capital ships searching for the *Bismarck*. Several vessels from Force H at Gibraltar, including the *Ark Royal* and *Renown*, also joined in the hunt. In a moment of pure farce, on the night of 26 May, Swordfish aircraft spotted and attacked the cruiser *Sheffield* in error. Thankfully none of their torpedoes hit home.

Opposite bottom: A second launch of aircraft from the *Ark Royal* attacked the German battleship later that evening. One of their torpedoes damaged the *Bismarck*'s rudder and brought her to a virtual stop. Able to steam only in circles, the end was not far away.

The *Renown* pennant, given to the battlecruiser and her crew for their part in the sinking of the *Bismarck*.

The Italian cruiser *Zara*, sunk at the Battle of Cape Matapan.

A silk postcard from HMS *King George V*.

H.M.A.C. **FORMIDABLE**
Aircraft Carrier, ILLUSTRIOUS Class. Completed 1941. Length 753ft.
Beam 95ft. Displacement 23,000 tons. Armament sixteen 4.5-inch guns.
110,000 h.p. Speed 32 knots. Complement 1,600.

The carrier *Formidable*, newly completed in 1941.

The *Bismarck*, the might of the German navy.

A Sunderland flying boat on patrol over the Western Approaches.

A British battlecruiser at sea.

There'll always Be An England

HER SONS ARE
    BRAVE AND FREE,
THEY FIGHT A
    RIGHTEOUS CAUSE
O'ER SKY, O'ER LAND
    AND SEA!

Left: HMS *Warspite*, Cunningham's flagship in the Mediterranean.

Below: A patriotic postcard from the early days of the war.

H.M.S. Warspite Battleship Queen Elizabeth class. *Length overall 644', beam (outside bulges) 104', draught 30' 8", displacement 30,600 tons, propelling machinery 80,000 s.h.p. turbines, screws 4, speed 24 knots, main armament 8–15", 8–6", 8–4" AA guns, 4 aircraft, complement 1,124, built Devonport Dockyard, lauched 1913.*

Above: A U-boat sinks a British merchant ship.

Disaster at Pearl Harbor. A close-up view of a sunken American battleship.

The Spirit of BRITAIN

WE SHALL GO ON TO THE END....WE SHALL FIGHT IN FRANCE, WE SHALL FIGHT ON THE SEAS AND IN, THE OCEANS, SHALL FIGHT WITH GROWING CONFIDENCE AND GROWING STRENGTH IN THE AIR.. WE SHALL DEFEND OUR ISLAND, WHATEVER THE COST MAY BE. WE SHALL FIGHT ON THE BEACHES, WE SHALL FIGHT ON THE LANDING GROUNDS, WE SHALL FIGHT IN THE FIELDS AND STREETS AND IN THE HILLS.... WE SHALL NEVER SURRENDER, AND EVEN IF, WHICH I DO NOT FOR A MOMENT BELIEVE, THIS ISLAND, OR EVEN PART OF IT, IS SUBJUGATED AND STARVING, THEN OUR EMPIRE ACROSS THE SEAS, ARMED AND GUARDED BY THE BRITISH FLEET, WILL CARRY ON THE STRUGGLE, UNTIL, IN GOD'S GOOD TIME, THE NEW WORLD, IN ALL ITS STRENGTH AND MIGHT, SETS FORTH TO THE RESCUE AND LIBERATION OF THE OLD. BRITAIN WILL FIGHT THE MENACE OF TYRANNY FOR YEARS, AND, IF NECESSARY, ALONE.

— WINSTON CHURCHILL

H.M.S. Ark Royal Aircraft carrier. Length overall 800', beam 94' 9", draught 22' 9", displacement 22,000 tons, propelling machinery 102,000 s.h.p. turbines, screws 3, speed 30½ knots, main armament 16–4·5", 48–2 pdr AA guns, 72 aircraft, complement 1,575, built Cammell Laird, launched 1937.

Above: HMS *Ark Royal*, the pride of the Royal Navy.

Opposite page: Churchill's famous words reproduced on a postcard.

Left: The Liberty ship *Jeremiah O'Brien*, one of hundreds built in the USA.

Below: A pre-war shot of the *Empress of Britain*.

The *Bismarck* took a terrible pounding from the guns of the *Rodney* and *King George V* – proof of the quality of her construction. Eventually, however, torpedoes from the cruisers *Norfolk* and *Dorsetshire*, together with the German crew, who set explosive charges against her hull, finished her off. The giant ship turned over and sank.

Opposite bottom: The mighty *King George V*, a vessel bristling with heavy guns and capable of making 30 knots; she was one of several battleships detailed to make an end of the *Bismarck*.

Fleet Air Arm pilots and aircrew from the *Ark Royal*, men who were decorated for their part in the destruction of the *Bismarck*, pose happily for the photographer.

Opposite top: Casualties of the war at sea in an African harbour.

Opposite bottom: An artist's impression of the sinking of the *Bismarck*.

Winston Churchill visiting Admiral Tovey at a northern naval base.

June

The French *Dunkerque*, a modern vessel that, in the hands of the Vichy French, represented a serious threat to British naval power in the Mediterranean.

The U-boat war continues – this shows a surfaced German submarine putting a torpedo into a lone merchantman.

Opposite top: The HMS *Nelson* at sea.

Opposite bottom: A crew inspection aboard the HMS *Prince of Wales*.

H. M. S. NELSON.

On 22 June, Britain was thrown a sudden and unexpected lifeline when Hitler launched Operation Barbarossa, his fateful attack on Russia. Initially, the German assault was successful right along the line, but gradually Russian stubbornness – and the terrible Russian winter – began to cause the Germans great losses. This shows German troops crossing the Russian border on the morning of 22 June.

The sloop *Auckland* was lost off Tobruk on 24 June. The Australian ship *Parramatta* rescued many of her crew, but some were machine-gunned by German aircraft as they swam to safety.

An artist's impression of a trawler sinking a Nazi U-boat.

Above: The RNAS destroyer *Waterham* – shown here in port – was sunk by German aircraft off Sallum on 29 June. She was the first Australian vessel to be sunk in the war.

Opposite top: The submarine *Parthian* attacked and sank the Free French *Souffleur* off Beirut on 25 June. The *Parthian* was herself later lost, probably as a result of hitting a mine.

Opposite bottom: The German weather ship *Lauenberg* was stopped in the Atlantic on 28 June. Before her crew were able to scuttle her, a number of valuable code books and Enigma components were taken from the German ship.

HMS *Valiant* and HMS *Barham* firing their 15-inch guns.

July

On 1 July, the RAF launched a series of attacks on Brest and its harbour. The heavy cruiser *Prinz Eugen*, recently part of Operation Rheinübung along with the *Bismarck*, was hit, causing serious damage to the ship and causing considerable damage. She was out of action for several months.

Royal Navy submarines lie alongside their depot ship. Already, by the middle of 1941, the value of the 'unseen killer' was obvious to all sides in the war.

The submarine *Utmost*, operating out of the besieged island of Malta, is shown here displaying her Jolly Roger as she returns to port after another successful mission. The white lines denote the number of ships the *Utmost* has sunk, the daggers show the 'special missions' in which she has been involved and the lifebuoy indicates the successful rescue on a ditched bomber crew.

On 25 July the cruiser *Newcastle* managed to intercept and damage the German ship *Erhangen*. The German vessel managed to scuttle herself before she could be boarded.

Italian motor boats, packed with explosives, attacked the Grand Harbour in Malta on 26 July. The Italian navy showed real expertise with innovative craft like these and with the two-man torpedoes which accompanied the motor boats in their attack on 26 June.

A Navy warship covered in ice after patrolling the northern waters.

August

In the first operational success for a catapult ship, a Sea Hurricane was launched on 3 August from the *Maplin*, formerly the *Erin*, and brought down a Focke-Wulf Condor reconnaissance aircraft. The pilot, Lt R. W. H. Everett, baled out of his aircraft once the Condor was despatched and was picked up from the sea. For his exploit Everett was awarded the DSO.

S.S. "AGUILA".

The giant Focke Wolfe Condors had an enormous range, flying from captured French airfields on the Atlantic coast. They were used to locate as well as attack convoys in-bound for Britain. The use of CAM ships flying off fighters was, for a long while, the only defence against these powerful aircraft that the convoys had.

Opposite top: Convoy OG-71 left the Mersey on 13 August and on the 18th was attacked by a U-boat wolf pack off the coast of Ireland. The commodore's ship, *Aguila* (shown here in a pre-war shot), was torpedoed and went down in just ninety seconds. She was carrying ninety service personnel, twenty WRNS among them, but only the ship's master and nine others were saved. Tragically, they later drowned when the rescue tug *Empire Oak* was sunk by the same wolf pack.

Opposite bottom: Anti-aircraft guns – pom-poms as they were called – were an effective means of defence for ships, but only against planes flying at low altitude.

The fast minelayer *Manxman* left England disguised as the French cruiser *Leopard* on 17 August. Flying the tricolour and with her crew dressed in French uniforms, by the 25th of the month she was laying mines in the Gulf of Genoa. She then retired at high speed and was back in the UK by the 30th.

It was not just merchant ships that were at risk from U-boats. The corvette *Picotee* was one of several escorts sunk in 1941 while guarding a convoy. She was torpedoed by *U-568* while protecting convoy N-54.

ARMS FOR RUSSIA . . . A great convoy of British ships escorted by Soviet fighter planes sails into Murmansk harbour with vital supplies for the Red Army.

With Russia now an ally of Britain, convoys began to run to Archangel carrying weapons and supplies. This poster proclaims the need to help Russia, but, in reality, how much aid was required and how much use was made of the tanks and guns that were transported has always been open to debate. The first Russian convoy left Iceland for Archangel on 21 August and, unlike future convoys, got through without enemy attack.

The Russian convoys saw some of the bitterest conflicts of the whole war – the enemy was not just the German U-boats and aircraft but also the weather. Ice and snow could make a ship top heavy and the danger of capsizing was ever-present. Torpedoed sailors had little chance of survival as thirty seconds of immersion in the freezing waters around northern Scandinavia and a man would be dead from hypothermia. This shows ice forming on a signal lamp on the cruiser *Sheffield*.

On 27 August, *U-570* was forced to the surface off Iceland and captured after an attack by an RAF Hudson. Brought into port, a complete Enigma decoding machine was discovered on board. The *U-570* was commissioned into the Royal Navy, sailing as HMS *Graph*.

The liner *Bremen* – shown here with her sister ship *Europa* – was once the pride of all Germany, a ship of great elegance and holder of the Blue Riband. In 1941 she was burned out while tied up at her deck in Bremerhaven – not an act of war but arson committed by a crewman who had a grudge against the owners. The *Bremen* had, since 1939, been used as a barrack ship and there had been plans that, if the invasion of Britain was ever launched, she would be used to transport soldiers. Her destruction ended all such speculation.

A sailor on a Royal Navy trawler. Their duties included minesweeping and hunting U-boats.

September

A convoy sets sail – unglamorous but vital work.

The Italian submarine *Scire* carried two-man torpedoes across the Mediterranean and, on 20 September, launched them against shipping moored in Gibraltar harbour. The attack was largely ineffective but the courage of the Italian sailors and divers was never in doubt.

A captured Italian two-man torpedo or chariot is seen here on display. The explosive charge, or warhead, at the front of the torpedo would have been enough to cause serious damage to any ship. The men who piloted the chariots were undoubtedly expendable, but the Italians had no difficulty recruiting men to carry out what were, in many respects, suicide missions.

When, on 21 September, a Martlet aircraft shot down a Focke-Wulf Condor attacking Convoy OG-74, it was the first success by a plane flown from one of the new auxiliary aircraft carriers that had just come into use. Built, in the main, in the USA and passed on to Britain as part of the Lend-Lease agreement, these vessels were also known as 'Woolworth Carriers' by the men of the Royal Navy.

The battleship *Malaya* ploughs steadily through a heavy sea.

Opposite top: The first British auxiliary carrier was the *Audacity*, a converted merchantman that showed the value of air cover for convoys. The escort carriers were smaller and less well armed than fleet carriers, but they were cheap and quick to build.

Opposite bottom: Operation Halberd was a convoy of nine 15-knot merchant ships that set out for the beleaguered island of Malta on 24 September. Escorted by cruisers like the *Edinburgh* and *Eurylus* and – from a distance – by battleships *Nelson* and *Rodney* – the convoy reached its destination on the 28th of the month.

A Coastal Command patrol.

October

On 2 October 1941, the keel of the *Vanguard* was laid down at John Brown's yard on the Clyde. She was destined to be Britain's largest and last battleship.

The destroyer *Broadwater*, previously the US navy ship *Mason*, was torpedoed and sunk by *U-101* in the Atlantic on 18 October. The old 'four stackers' sold by the USA to Britain were virtually obsolete even before the deal was begun, but they carried out heroic and vital duties on the convoy routes. Several of them were sunk in the course of those duties.

Convoys across the Mediterranean to bring vital supplies to Malta were both dangerous and dogged. This shows a merchant vessel being straddled by bombs.

When Admiral Sir James Somerville was appointed KBE on 21 October, it brought an immediate response from his colleague Admiral Cunningham. Somerville was already a KCB and Cunningham, on hearing the news, signalled: 'What, twice a night at your age?'

Left: Submarines were effective weapons of war, well deployed by all sides, but they were cramped and conditions inside their hulls were unpleasant, as this view of the control room of the *Utmost* clearly shows.

Below: A Free French submarine being inspected by Admiral Musélier.

HMS *Rodney* in the Grand Harbour at Malta. The siege of Malta lasted many months, thousands of houses being destroyed and many civilians killed. The bravery of the Maltese people was recognised by the award of the George Cross to the whole island.

The bombardment of a supply base in North Africa.

Opposite top: The destroyer *Cossack*, famous for her part in the 'Altmark Affair', was torpedoed on 23 October while escorting Convoy HG-75. Taken in tow, it was originally hoped she could be saved. It was not to be and she sank off Cape St Vincent on 27 October.

Opposite bottom: As 1941 drew to a close, the Russian convoys continued to cause suffering for both Royal and Merchant Navy seamen. Ice on deck was a perpetual problem – no-one wanted to find themselves in the freezing water.

The 16-inch shells of HMS *Nelson*.

November

The *Valiant*, one of several powerful battleships stationed in the Mediterranean, either with Force H or with Cunningham's Mediterranean fleet.

The Germans claimed to have sunk her many times, but the end finally came for the aircraft carrier *Ark Royal* off Gibraltar on 13–14 November. Torpedoed by *U 81* on the 13th, most of the crew were evacuated before she finally slipped below the waves the next day.

An action photograph of the crew of *Ark Royal* abandoning ship. Efforts to save the giant carrier had proved inadequate – now, with hindsight, it seems that with better damage control, she might have been saved.

Admiral Sir Percy Noble succeeded Sir Martin Dunbar-Nasmith as Commander-in-Chief of Western Approaches on 17 November.

In a bizarre encounter in the Indian Ocean on 19 November, the RNAS cruiser *Sydney* and the German raider *Kormoran* sank each other. The *Kormoran* apparently approached the unsuspecting Australian ship with no guns or flags showing. Australian sailors were lounging at the rails – and then the raider opened fire at point blank range and with devastating results.

The *Sydney* managed to reply with a few accurate rounds before she heeled away, blazing furiously. She sank without trace and with no survivors.

Right: The *Sydney* might have been taken by surprise, but with the few rounds that hit the German ship it was clear that the *Kormoran* was also mortally wounded. In total, 315 of her crew were rescued before she sank.

Below: By the end of 1941, the day of the surface raider was almost over. As if to prove the point, the *Atlantis* was discovered and sunk by the *Devonshire* in the South Atlantic on 22 November. From now on, U-boats would have to shoulder the burden of commerce raiding.

Merchant shipping under fire in a Malta convoy, a photograph taken from HMS *Manchester*.

An aerial view of the carrier *Illustrious*.

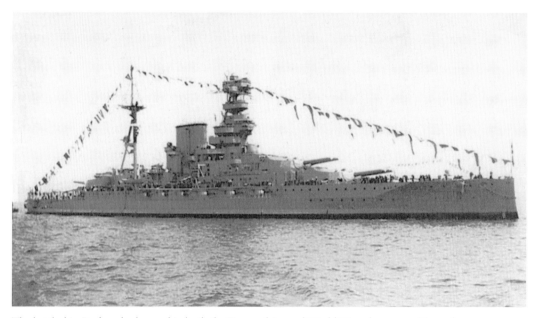

The battleship *Barham* had served in both the First and Second World Wars, but on 25 November 1941, she was hit by torpedoes from *U-331* and blew up in less than five minutes. Out of her total crew only 450 survived, 862 being lost in the disaster.

The moment of destruction – the explosion that destroyed the *Barham* is caught in this remarkable and dramatic photograph. The *Barham* was the first battleship lost in open sea since the sinking of the *Britannia* in 1918.

The beautiful sleek lines of the Italian cruiser *Conti de Cavour* can be clearly seen in this photograph – small wonder Mussolini was proud of his navy.

In this photograph, fuses of depth charges are being set, while a Coastal Command aircraft flies in the background.

December

Admiral Hipper, the German pocket battleship, was another Axis ship with sleek and beautiful lines.

As a way of countering potential Japanese expansion in the Far East, at the end of November 1941, the Admiralty despatched the battleship *Prince of Wales*, the battlecruiser *Repulse* and several smaller craft to Singapore. This was Force Z under Admiral Sir Tom Phillips. The ships arrived at Singapore on 2 December.

Japanese aircraft line the flight deck of the carrier *Kaga*, used in the attack on Pearl Harbor on the morning of Sunday 7 December. The attack on Pearl Harbor took America and the entire world by surprise. In fact, a coded Japanese message, effectively declaring war, had been sent to Washington – it was not relayed to Hawaii until midday, by which time the attack had already taken place. The 'day of infamy' brought the USA into the war, not just against Japan but also Germany.

Japanese pilots pose happily for the camera on the deck of their carrier.

GALATEA

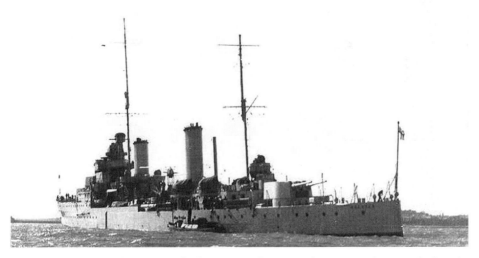

With the situation in the Far East looking pretty desperate, things were almost as bad in the Mediterranean. On 14 December, the cruiser *Galatea* was sunk by the *U-557*, operating in the waters off Alexandria.

Japanese pilots stand en masse for a briefing before setting off on the mission to attack the American Pacific Fleet at Pearl.

The escort carrier *Audacity* was torpedoed and sunk by *U-751* on 21 December, 500 miles west of Cape Finisterre.

Admiral Isoruku Yamamoto, architect of the attack on Pearl Harbor. He had few illusions about the course of the war, declaring that he might 'run wild' for the first year or so, but, eventually, defeat was inevitable. Although he may well have thought it, there is no record of Yamamoto ever declaring that the attack had simply 'awoken a sleeping giant'.

Japanese A6M2 aircraft on the deck of the *Akagi* before the attack began.

Opposite top: The Japanese carrier *Kaga* is seen here from the air.

Opposite bottom: Japanese aircraft attack Pearl Harbor a few minutes before 8.00 a.m. on 7 December. Most of the servicemen were still asleep in their barracks or on board ship. A total of 184 Japanese aircraft from six carriers raced in at low altitude, followed by a second wave of 171 torpedo bombers, taking the defenders totally by surprise and encountering almost no opposition.

With no fear of attack – or even the inclination that such a thing might happen – the Americans had made little preparation. Aircraft were lined up in rows on the tarmac airfields and the ships in 'Battleship Row' stretched out in neat, symmetrical lines. They made a perfect target for the Japanese bombers.

Opposite top: All eight battleships in 'Battleship Row' were hit and five were sunk at their moorings. Three cruisers and three destroyers were also sunk, a total of 2,043 men being killed along with a further 1,000 who were injured.

Opposite bottom: The battleship *Arizona*, sunk but still on fire several hours after the attack had ended.

An aerial view of the American carrier *Yorktown*. By sheer luck, the three American aircraft carriers that had been one of the principal targets for Yamamoto's bombers were absent from harbour on the morning of 7 December. If they had been present, they would have been highly vulnerable. In all probability they would have been destroyed and the whole course of the war would have been different.

Opposite top: Zero fighters line the deck of the carrier *Shokaku*, waiting their turn to take off and attack the American fleet. Admiral Nagumo failed to launch a third wave to take out the oil tanks at Pearl Harbor, possibly because, with the whole area wreathed in smoke, he thought they had already been hit. It was a major oversight.

Opposite bottom: The *Nevada* on fire, attempting to get out of Pearl and find sanctuary in the open sea.

Admiral Sir Tom Phillips, with Rear Admiral Palliser, the men in charge of Force Z. In the wake of the attack on Pearl Harbor the Japanese made air attacks on Wake Island and landings at various places in Malaya and Thailand. In an attempt to prevent further landings on the Malaysian peninsula, the *Prince of Wales* and *Repulse* left Singapore on 8 December. They had destroyer escorts but no air cover whatsoever.

The two British capital ships under attack. Their destruction left the British naval presence in the area at absolute zero.

The *Prince of Wales* sinking.

Japanese G4M-50 'Betty' bombers from the Kanaga Air Group, the type of plane that attacked and sank the *Prince of Wales* and *Repulse*.

The *Moth* as *Suma*, now in the service of the Japanese navy.

With the Japanese naval and military forces triumphant virtually everywhere in the Far East, Britain and the newly involved Americans found themselves in a desperate position. British and American colonies and territories were under immediate threat and it was not at all clear how they were going to be defended. On 12 December, the gunboat *Moth* was scuttled as a blockship in the harbour at Hong Kong. She was later raised and commissioned into the Japanese navy as the *Suma*, only to be sunk by an American mine on 19 March 1945.

On 19 December, three Italian midget submarines managed to slip through the boom defence network at Alexandria and lay charges against the hulls of the battleships *Queen Elizabeth* and *Valiant*. When the charges exploded, both ships were grievously hurt. They settled slowly into the shallow waters and were out of action for many months.

With Hong Kong under attack, on the day before Christmas the gunboat *Robin* was scuttled in the harbour to avoid capture. It was a forlorn gesture as the Japanese were already at the gates and surrender was only a matter of time.

Hong Kong surrendered to the Japanese on Christmas Day 1941. This shows the victorious Japanese marching through the town, led by Lt-General Takashi Sakai and Vice Admiral Masaichi Niimi. It was the end of a very bad year for Britain.